My 2 in 1 Picture Dictionary

A to Z pages

make believe ideas

Aa

ambulance
An **ambulance** is a special van that is used to take people to hospital when they are hurt or ill.

animal
An **animal** is something that lives and moves around. A plant is not an animal. Cats, robins, spiders, and goldfish are all animals.

Nee naa! Nee naa!

aeroplane
An **aeroplane** is a flying machine with wings that carries people and things.

alphabet
An **alphabet** is the letters that are used in writing, arranged in a special order.

angry
If you are **angry**, you feel very upset and annoyed.

apple
An **apple** is a round, juicy fruit that grows on a tree. Its skin can be green, red, or yellow.

Bb

basket
A **basket** is a container used to store and carry things.

bee
A **bee** is an insect with wings. Bees make honey.

ball
A **ball** is a round object used in games. You throw, catch, hit, or kick a ball.

bat
A **bat** is a piece of wood that is used to hit a ball in a game.

beetle
A **beetle** is an insect that has hard, shiny wings.

banana
A **banana** is a long fruit with a thick, yellow skin.

bed
A **bed** is something you lie down and sleep on.

bicycle
A **bicycle** is a machine you ride. It has two wheels and pedals.

A B C D E F G H I J K L M N O P Q R S T U V W X Y Z

bird
A **bird** is an animal with wings, feathers, and a beak. Most birds can fly.

book
A **book** is made up of pages held together inside a cover.

box
A **box** is used to keep things in. Most boxes are made of cardboard.

body
The **body** of a person or an animal is every part of them.

bottle
A **bottle** holds liquids. Bottles are usually made of glass or plastic.

boy
A **boy** is a child who will grow up to be a man.

bowl
A **bowl** is a deep dish that holds food like soup, breakfast cereal, or fruit.

bread
Bread is a food made with flour. It is baked in an oven.

bucket
A **bucket** is used to carry liquid.

butterfly
A **butterfly** is an insect that has four large wings.

broccoli
Broccoli is a green vegetable.

bulldozer
A **bulldozer** is a big machine that pushes rocks out of the way.

brush
A **brush** has lots of stiff hairs or wires. Most brushes have a handle.

bus
A **bus** is a long vehicle with seats inside to carry people around.

button
A **button** is a small object that you sew on to clothes to fasten them.

Cc

carrot
A **carrot** is a long, orange vegetable that grows under the ground.

caterpillar
A **caterpillar** looks like a worm with legs. It turns into a butterfly or moth.

cake
A **cake** is a sweet food. It is made by mixing butter, sugar, eggs, and flour and baking it in an oven.

cat
A **cat** is an animal with soft fur, sharp claws, and a long tail. People keep small cats as pets.

chair
A **chair** is a seat with four legs and a back.

car
A **car** is a machine with four wheels and an engine.

catch
When you **catch** something, you take hold of it while it is moving.

cheese
Cheese is a food made from milk.

child

A **child** is a young boy or girl. When there is more than one child, they are called children.

clock

A **clock** is a machine that shows you what time it is.

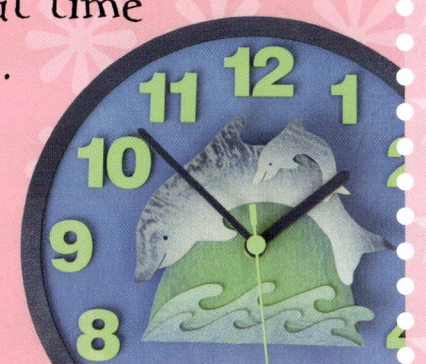

clown

A **clown** is someone who says and does funny things to make people laugh.

clothes

Clothes are the things that people wear, such as trousers, dresses, and shirts.

colour

Red, blue, and yellow are **colours**. By mixing them together, you get other colours.

chocolate

Chocolate is a sweet, brown food made from cocoa beans.

comb

A **comb** is a piece of plastic or metal that has lots of thin teeth. You use a comb to tidy your hair.

computer

A **computer** is a machine that stores information and can work things out.

crawl

When you **crawl**, you move around on your hands and knees.

cry

When you **cry**, tears fall from your eyes.

cow

A **cow** is a large female farm animal that produces milk. The male animal is called a bull. The baby is called a calf.

Moo!

crocodile

A **crocodile** is an animal with sharp teeth, short legs, and a long tail.

cucumber

A **cucumber** is a long, green vegetable.

crown

A **crown** is a kind of hat, usually worn by kings and queens. It's often made of gold or silver.

cup

A **cup** is a small, round container with a handle. You drink from a cup.

Dd

dish
A **dish** is a bowl for serving food.

dog
A **dog** is an animal that barks. Dogs are often kept as pets.

dice
Dice are small cubes that have a different number of spots on each side.

doctor
A **doctor** takes care of people who are sick or hurt and helps them to get better.

dinosaur
Dinosaurs were large animals that lived on Earth millions of years ago.

donkey
A **donkey** is a furry animal that looks like a small horse with long ears.

Ee

egg
Birds, fish, snakes, and lizards live inside eggs until they are big enough to hatch out.

envelope
An **envelope** is a paper cover for a letter or a card.

eagle
An **eagle** is a large bird with big wings, a curved beak, and sharp claws.

elephant
An **elephant** is a large, grey animal that has big ears and a long nose, called a trunk.

exercise
When you **exercise**, you move your body to keep fit.

ear
Your **ears** are on each side of your head. You hear with your ears.

eye
Your **eyes** are on your face. You see with your eyes.

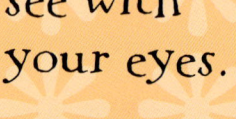

Ff

family
Your **family** is the group of people that are closest to you. Your Mum, Dad, brothers, and sisters are all part of your family.

feather
Birds have **feathers** on their body to keep them warm and dry. Feathers can also help birds fly.

face
Your **face** is the front part of your head. Your eyes, nose, and mouth are all part of your face.

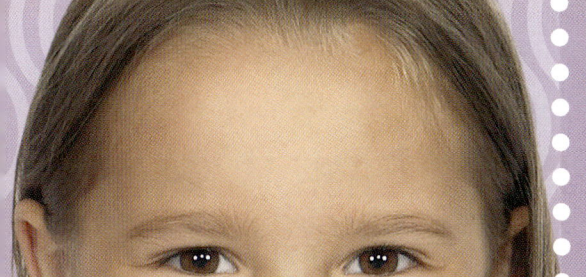

finger
Your **fingers** are part of your hand. Each hand has four fingers and a thumb.

farm
A **farm** is a place where farmers grow food and keep animals.

fire
A **fire** is the hot, bright flames and smoke made when something is burning.

fire engine

A **fire engine** is a special vehicle with a ladder and water hoses. Firefighters use fire engines to drive to fires and put them out.

Nee naa! Nee naa!

flower

A **flower** is part of a plant. Flowers are often perfumed and brightly coloured.

fork

A **fork** has sharp prongs and a handle. You use a small fork for eating and a big fork for digging in the garden.

food

Food is all the different things you eat to keep you fit and healthy.

frog

A **frog** is a small animal that lives in ponds and damp places.

fish

A **fish** is an animal that lives in water. Fish are covered in scales and have gills for breathing under water.

fruit

A **fruit** is the part of a plant that holds the seeds. Lots of fruits, like apples and grapes, are juicy and good to eat.

Gg

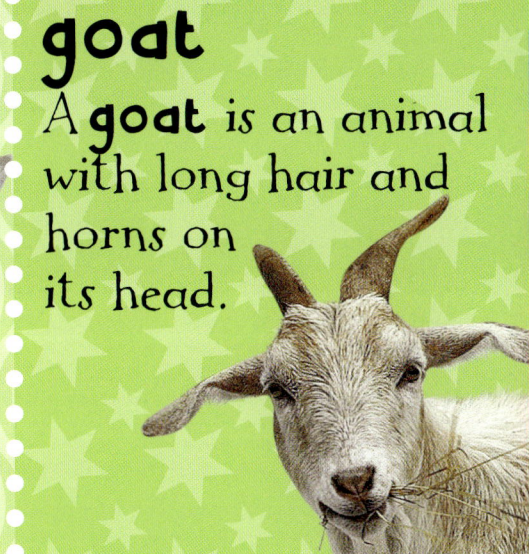

game
A **game** is something you play for fun. Bat and ball is a game.

gate
A **gate** is a kind of door in a wall, fence, or hedge.

giraffe
A **giraffe** is a tall animal with long legs and a very long neck.

girl
A **girl** is a child who will grow up to be a woman.

goat
A **goat** is an animal with long hair and horns on its head.

grape
A **grape** is a small, purple or green fruit that grows in bunches. Grapes are used to make wine.

grow
When somebody or something grows, it gets bigger.

Hh

head
Your **head** is the part of your body that is above your neck.

hop
You **hop** when you jump up and down on one leg.

half
A **half** is one of two pieces that are equal in size.

helicopter
A **helicopter** is a flying machine with spinning blades that let it take off straight up from the ground and hover. Helicopters don't have wings.

horse
A **horse** is a big animal with hooves. People ride horses and use them to pull loads.

hammer
A **hammer** is a tool for knocking nails into wood.

house
A **house** is a building where people live.

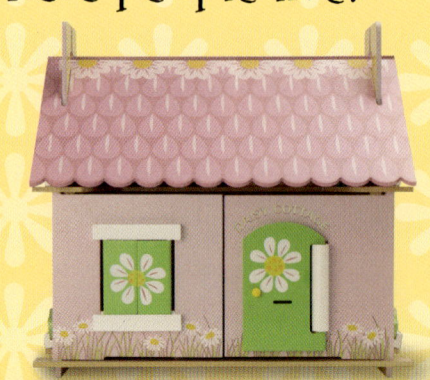

Ii

Jj

idea
An **idea** is something you think of.

ice
Ice is made when water freezes. Ice is very cold and hard.

insects
An **insect** is a small animal with six legs. Many insects have wings. Butterflies, flies, and beetles are all insects.

jar
Jars are usually made of glass. They are used for keeping foods, like jam, fresh.

ice cream
Ice cream is a sweet, creamy, frozen food.

jewel
A **jewel** is a beautiful, sparkling stone. Some jewels, like diamonds, cost a lot of money.

Kk

jigsaw
A **jigsaw** is a puzzle made from lots of pieces that you can fit together to make a picture.

juice
Juice is the liquid that comes out of fruit when you squeeze it.

key
A **key** is a specially shaped piece of metal that is used to lock or unlock a door.

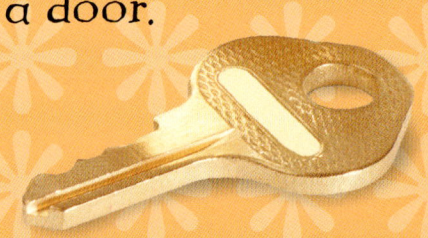

king
A **king** is a man who is born to rule a country. A queen's husband is also called a king.

jump
When you **jump**, you lift both feet off the ground and move suddenly up into the air.

kick
When you **kick** something, you hit it with your foot.

knife
A **knife** is a tool used for cutting. Most knives have a handle and a long, sharp metal blade.

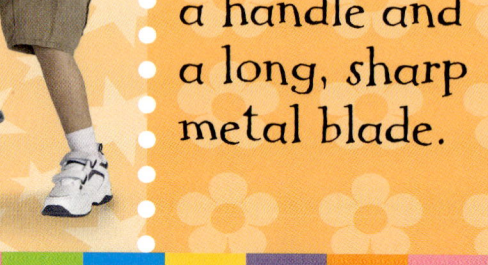

Ll

lamp
A **lamp** gives you light. You can move a lamp around and switch it on and off.

letter
A **letter** is a sign you use to write words. A, m, and z are all letters.

A **letter** is also a message that you write on paper to someone.

ladder
A **ladder** is used for climbing up high. Ladders are made of metal or wood.

leaf
A **leaf** is one of the flat, green parts of a plant or tree.

lamb
A **lamb** is a young sheep that is still with its mother.

lemon
A **lemon** is a juicy, yellow fruit with a sour taste.

lion
A **lion** is a big, wild cat. Lions live in Africa and India.

Mm

map
A **map** is a drawing that shows you where places are, so you can find your way around.

medicine
When you are ill, you take **medicine** to make you well again.

man
A **man** is a grown-up male person.

mask
A **mask** is something that you wear to cover your face. People wear masks to change the way they look.

milk
Milk is a white liquid that mother animals make to feed their babies with. Many people drink cows' milk.

mirror
A **mirror** is a sheet of special glass that you can see yourself in.

money
Money is the notes and coins that you use to buy things.

mountain
A **mountain** is a very high piece of land or rock.

mushroom
A **mushroom** is a plant that looks like a little umbrella. You can eat some mushrooms.

moon
The **moon** shines in the sky at night. It moves slowly around the Earth once a month.

mouse
A **mouse** is a small, furry animal with a long tail. Mice have sharp front teeth for gnawing food.

music
Music is the sound that people make when they sing and play instruments.

motorbike
A **motorbike** has two wheels and an engine.

mug
A **mug** is a large, straight cup with a handle. You drink hot drinks from a mug.

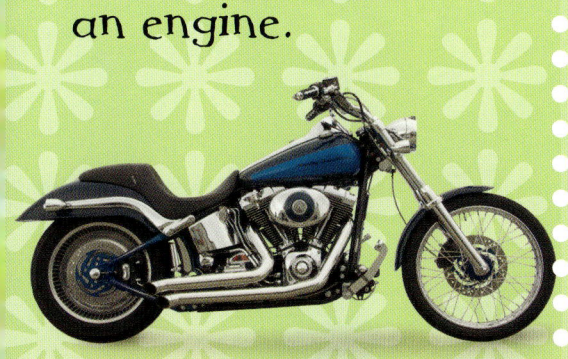

Nn

net
number
Numbers tell you how many of something you have. 3 and 100 are both numbers.

needle
A **needle** is a small, thin piece of metal used for sewing. It is sharp at one end and has a hole for thread at the other.

A **net** is made from pieces of string or thread tied together with holes in between. Nets are used for catching fish and also in games like tennis and football.

nurse
A **nurse** is a person who takes care of people who are ill or hurt. Nurses often work in hospitals.

nest
A **nest** is the home that animals like birds and mice make for their babies.

nose
Your **nose** is part of your face. You use it for breathing and smelling.

Oo

oven
An **oven** is the hot cupboard in a cooker where you roast or bake food.

opposite
An **opposite** is completely different. The opposite of full is empty.

owl
An **owl** is a bird that hunts for small animals at night. It has big eyes to help it see in the dark.

orange
An **orange** is a round, juicy fruit with thick, orange peel.

Pp

paint
Paint is a liquid that you put on to things to change the colour.

paper
Paper is a very thin material used for drawing and writing.

parrot

A **parrot** is a bird with brightly coloured feathers and a sharp, curved beak. Some parrots can talk.

pencil

A **pencil** is a long, thin stick of wood with black or coloured lead in the middle. Pencils are used for writing and drawing.

pet

A **pet** is a tame animal that you look after in your home. Cats, dogs, and hamsters are often kept as pets.

penguin

A **penguin** is a black-and-white sea bird that lives on cold coastlines. Penguins can't fly. They use their wings to swim.

pen

A **pen** is something you use to write or draw with in ink.

pig

A **pig** is an animal with a fat body, short legs, and a curly tail.

pirate

A **pirate** is a sailor who attacks and robs other sailors at sea.

plate

A **plate** is a flat dish that you put food on.

present

A **present** is something special that you give to someone to make them happy.

play

When you **play**, you have fun with your friends and join in games. Children and baby animals love to play with toys.

pumpkin

A **pumpkin** is a large fruit with orange skin.

plant

A **plant** is a living thing that grows in soil or water. Trees, flowers, and grass are all plants.

puppet

A **puppet** is a toy figure. You move a puppet by pulling strings or by putting your hand inside it.

Qq Rr

rainbow
A **rainbow** is an arch of bright colours that you see when the sun shines through rain.

queen
A **queen** is a woman who is born to rule a country.

rabbit
A **rabbit** is a small, furry animal with long ears and a tufty white tail.

read
When you **read**, you can understand words that are written down.

question
A **question** is what you ask when you want to know something.

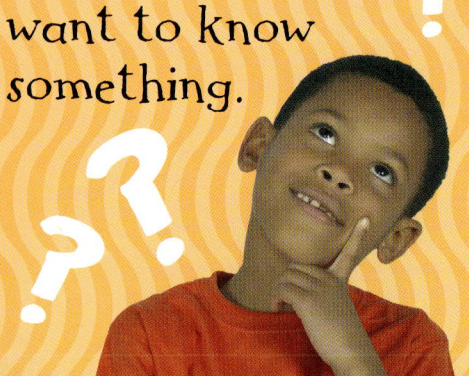

rain
Rain is lots of little drops of water that fall from the clouds.

rhinoceros
A **rhinoceros** is a big animal with tough, leathery skin and horns on its head.

Ss

robot
A **robot** is a machine that can do some of the jobs that people do.

saw
A **saw** is a tool with sharp, metal teeth for cutting through wood.

rocket
A **rocket** is the part of a spacecraft that pushes it high into space.

sandwich
A **sandwich** is made of two slices of bread with a filling, such as cheese or ham, between them.

scarf
You wear a **scarf** around your neck to keep you warm.

ruler
A **ruler** is a long, flat piece of wood or plastic that is used for drawing lines and measuring length.

saucepan
A **saucepan** is a deep, metal cooking pot with a handle and usually a lid.

scissors
A pair of **scissors** is a tool used for cutting paper or cloth. Scissors have two sharp blades and two handles.

screw

A **screw** is a thin, sharp piece of metal. You twist screws into pieces of wood to hold them together.

sheep

A **sheep** is an animal with a thick, woolly coat. Farmers keep sheep for their meat, wool, and milk.

ship

A **ship** is a big boat that carries people or things across the sea.

shape

The **shape** of something is its outline or the way it looks on the outside.

shoe

You wear **shoes** on your feet to protect them.

shark

A **shark** is a big sea fish. Some sharks have very sharp teeth and can attack people.

shell

A **shell** is a hard covering around something. Shellfish and nuts have shells.

sleep

When you **sleep**, you close your eyes and rest.

smile

When you **smile**, the corners of your mouth turn up. A smile shows you are feeling happy.

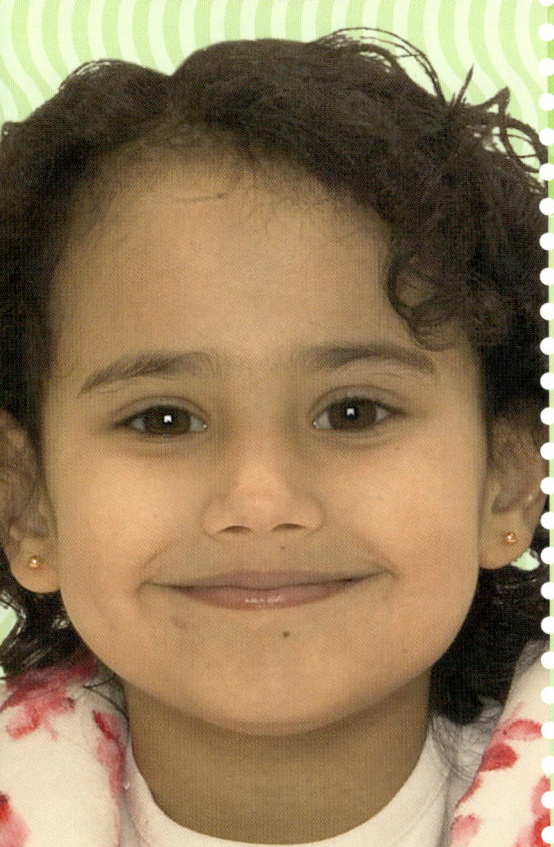

snowman

A **snowman** is the shape of a person made out of snow.

spider

A **spider** is a small animal with eight legs. Spiders spin webs to catch insects for food.

sock

You wear **socks** on your feet to keep them warm.

spoon

A **spoon** has a long handle and a round part at one end. You use a spoon to eat foods like soup and cereals.

snake

A **snake** has a long body and no legs. Its skin is made of scales.

spade

A **spade** is a tool used for digging holes in the ground. It has a long handle and a flat, metal end.

squirrel

A **squirrel** is a small, furry animal that lives in trees. It has a bushy tail and eats nuts.

stamp

A **stamp** is a small piece of paper that usually has a picture on it. You stick a stamp on a letter or parcel before posting it.

stool

A **stool** is a seat with legs but no back.

swan

A **swan** is a large bird with a long neck. It lives on rivers and lakes.

star

A **star** is a small, bright light in the sky. You can see stars on a clear, dark night. A star is also a shape with five or more points.

strawberry

A **strawberry** is a soft, sweet red fruit with seeds on it.

swing

starfish

A **starfish** is an animal that lives in the sea. It has five arms and looks like a star.

sun

The **sun** shines in the sky and gives the Earth light and heat. It is a star and the Earth moves around it.

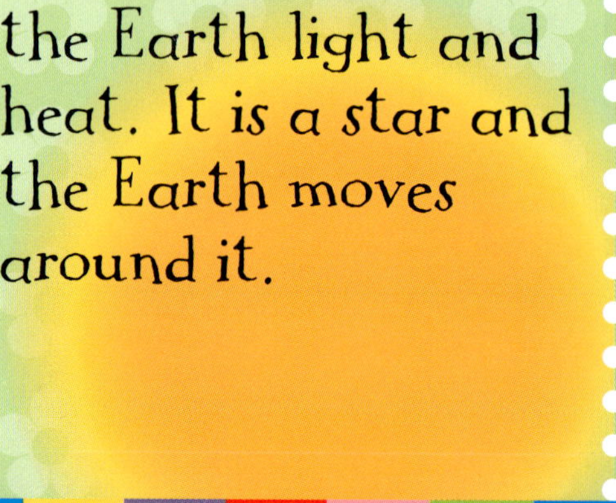

A **swing** is a seat hung on ropes or chains. It swings backwards and forwards.

Tt

telephone
A **telephone** is a machine you use to speak to someone in another place.

thermometer
You use a **thermometer** to find out how hot or cold something is.

table
A **table** is a piece of furniture with legs and a flat top. You can eat at a table.

tent
A **tent** is a shelter made out of a piece of cloth stretched over metal poles. You use a tent for camping.

tiger
A **tiger** is a big, wild cat with orange fur and black stripes. Wild tigers are rare, but some still live in India and China.

tail
An animal's **tail** grows at the end of its body.

tomato

A **tomato** is a soft, red, round fruit that you often eat in salads.

toothbrush

You use a **toothbrush** and toothpaste to clean your teeth.

tractor

A **tractor** is a farm vehicle with big back wheels to pull things.

tool

A **tool** is something that you hold in your hands to help you do a job. Saws, drills, and spades are all tools.

towel

A **towel** is a piece of soft, thick cloth that you use to dry yourself.

tree

A **tree** is a tall plant with leaves, branches, and a thick stem of wood called a trunk.

toy

A **toy** is a thing that a child plays with. Dolls, kites, and train sets are all toys.

truck

A **truck** is a strong vehicle often used to carry goods.

Uu Vv

vase
A **vase** is a kind of jar that is used to hold cut flowers.

umbrella
An **umbrella** keeps you dry when it rains.

vacuum cleaner
A **vacuum cleaner** is a machine that sucks up dust and dirt. 

vegetable
A **vegetable** is a plant that can be eaten raw or cooked. Carrots, cabbages, and onions are all vegetables.

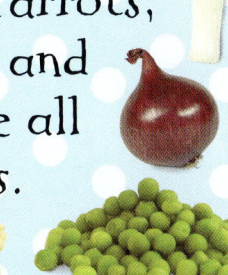

uniform
Some people wear **uniform** to show what job they do or which school they go to.

violin
A **violin** is a musical instrument made of wood. You play it using a bow.

A B C D E F G H I J K L M N O P Q R S T U V W X Y Z

Ww

wheel
Wheels are round and they can turn. Bicycles, cars, and trains all have wheels.

watch
A **watch** is a small clock that you wear on your wrist. It tells you what time it is.

woman
A **woman** is a grown-up female person.

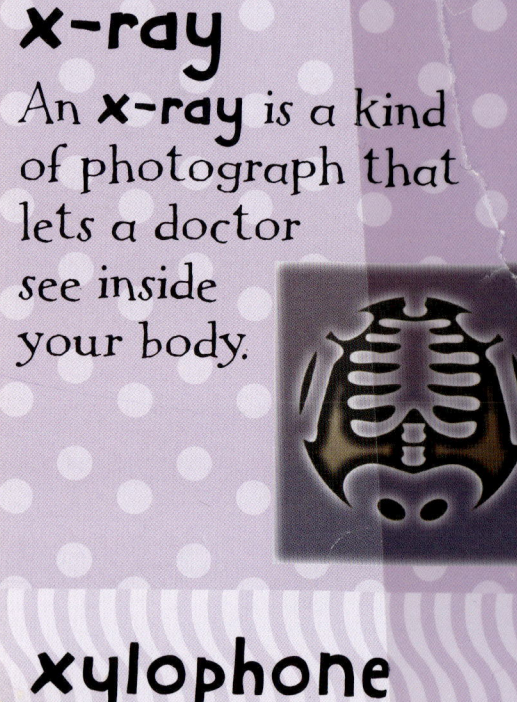

water
Water is the clear liquid in rivers, seas, and rain. Water also comes out of taps.

Xx

x-ray
An **x-ray** is a kind of photograph that lets a doctor see inside your body.

xylophone
A **xylophone** is a musical instrument with a row of wooden bars.

Yy

yoghurt
Yoghurt is a food made from milk. It is often mixed with sweet fruit.

Zz

yacht
A **yacht** is a boat with sails. Most yachts also have an engine.

yolk
The **yolk** is the yellow or orange middle part of an egg.

zebra
A **zebra** looks like a horse with black and white stripes. Zebras live in Africa.

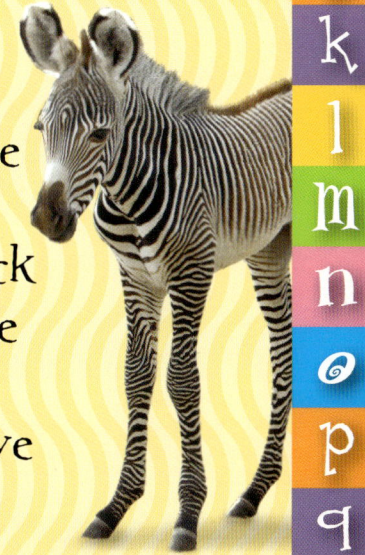

yawn
When you **yawn**, you open your mouth wide and breathe out noisily.

yo-yo
A **yo-yo** is a round toy that you roll up and down on a string.

zip
A **zip** joins two pieces of material together. A zip has two rows of teeth that lock together when you do it up.

100 one hundred buttons

10 ten paints

9 nine ducklings

8 eight flowers

5 five tomatoes

4 four spanners

3 three kittens

Numbers

Numbers tell you how many people or things there are. A number can be written as a word (one, two, three) or as a numeral (1, 2, 3).

1 one puppy

2 two babies

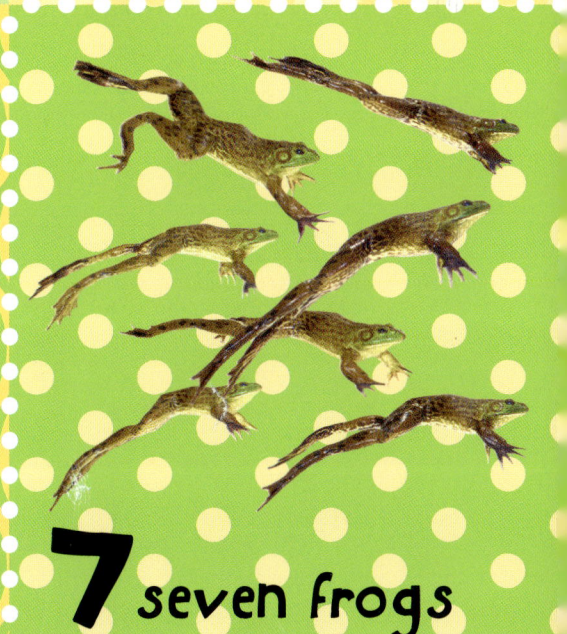

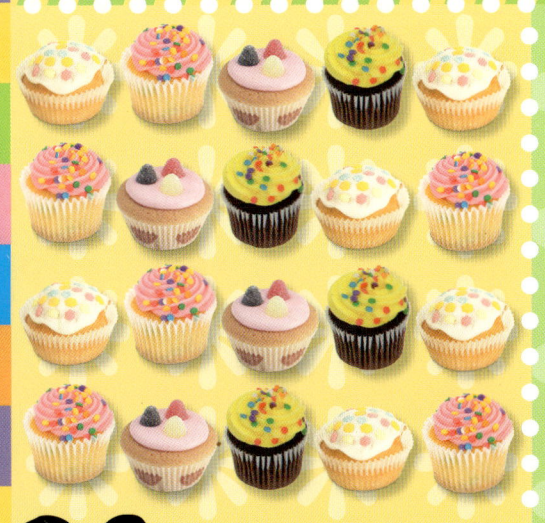

6 six tractors

7 seven frogs

20 twenty cakes

50 fifty jelly beans

full   empty

tall

fast

slow

thin

fat

short

new

old

open

shut

happy

sad

Opposites

When things are the **opposite** of each other, they are completely different. Tall is the opposite of short and hot is the opposite of cold.

asleep

awake

clean

dirty

dark

light

wet

dry

hot   cold

big

little

Colours

Red, blue, and yellow are **colours**. By mixing them together you can make other colours, such as green, purple, and orange.

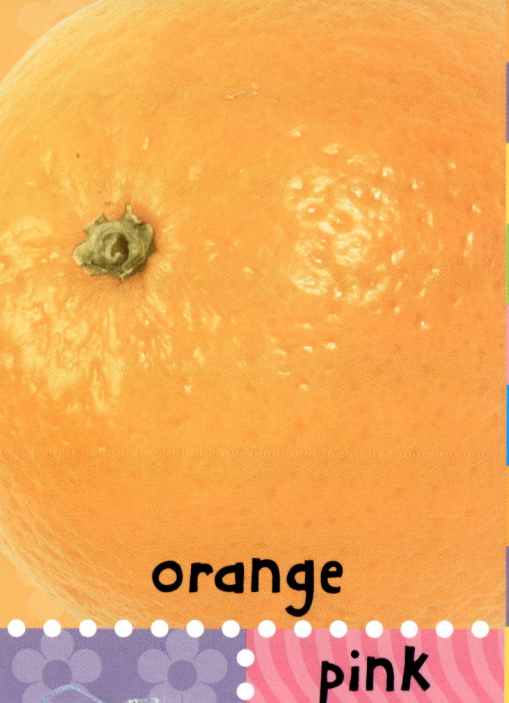

red

blue

yellow

green

orange

black

white

purple

pink

grey

brown

Shapes

A **shape** is the way an object looks on the outside, or the pattern you make when you draw around it. Circles, squares, and triangles are shapes.

circle

triangle

square

rectangle

cone

cylinder

star

heart

hexagon

pentagon

spiral

sphere

oval

cube

Time

Time is measured in minutes, hours, days, weeks, months, and years. The time is a particular moment in the day.

Months

January	July
February	August
March	September
April	October
May	November
June	December

Days of the week

Sunday
Monday
Tuesday
Wednesday
Thursday
Friday
Saturday

Seasons

Spring

Summer

Autumn

Winter

Telling the time

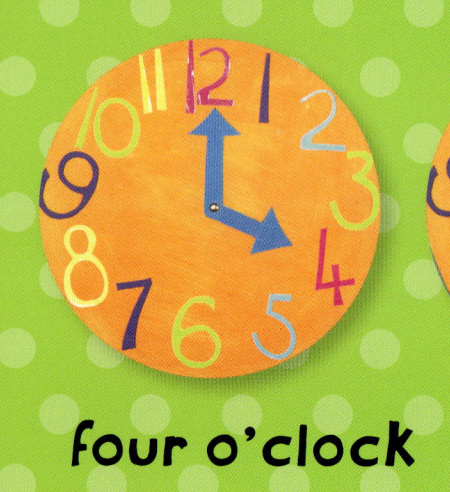

four o'clock   quarter past four   half past four   quarter to five

Doing words

Words that describe what we are doing are known as verbs. Most verbs describe actions, such as eating, drinking, reading, or jumping.

skipping

swinging

crouching

catching

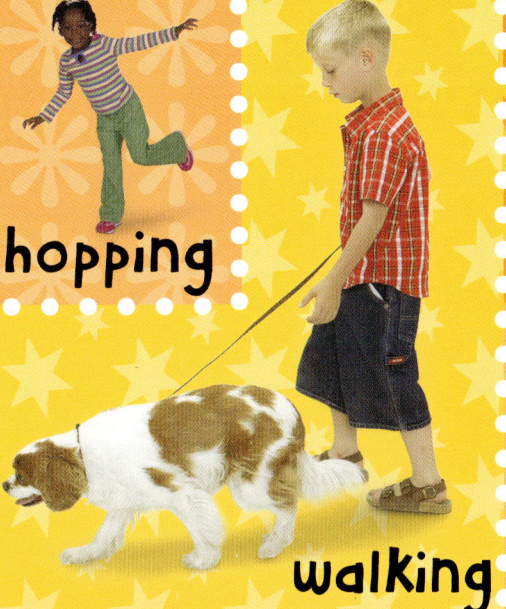

hopping

bathing

yawning

walking

crying

kissing

eating

hugging

crawling

rocket

bus

police car

boat

van

motorbike

bulldozer

dumper

fire engine

23

Things that go

Trucks, trains, buses, and cars carry people and goods on land. Boats travel on the sea, and planes and helicopters go through the air.

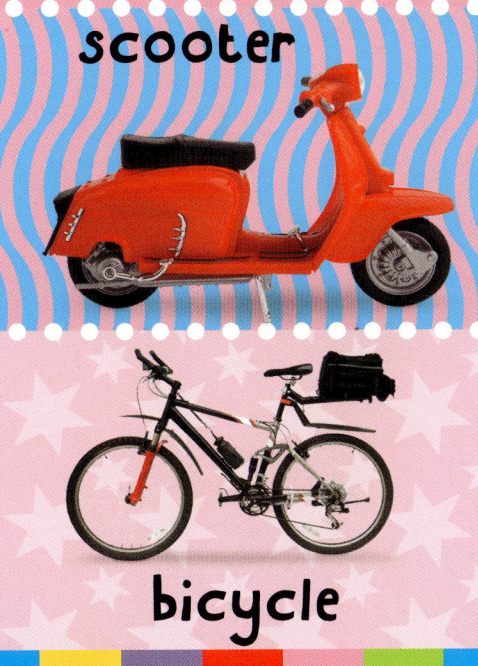

quad bike

car

helicopter

aeroplane

tractor

scooter

ambulance

bicycle

truck

Beach

A **beach** is the strip of land on the edge of the sea. Beaches are usually covered with sand or pebbles.

deckchair

boat

bucket

starfish

spade

swimsuit

windmill

shell

sandcastle

School

School is the place where you go to learn. At school, teachers teach children how to read, write, and count, and other important things.

violin

glue

recorder

paints

books

ruler

teacher

crayons

brush

triangle

paper

pen

tambourine

Tools

A **tool** is something you use to help you do a job. Hammers, saws, drills, spanners, and screwdrivers are all tools.

drill

scissors

spade

bucket

spanners

watering can

mallet

hammer

screwdrivers

trowel

saw

tool box

pliers

Toys

A **toy** is something you play with. Teddy bears, dolls, train sets, kites, and jigsaw puzzles are all toys.

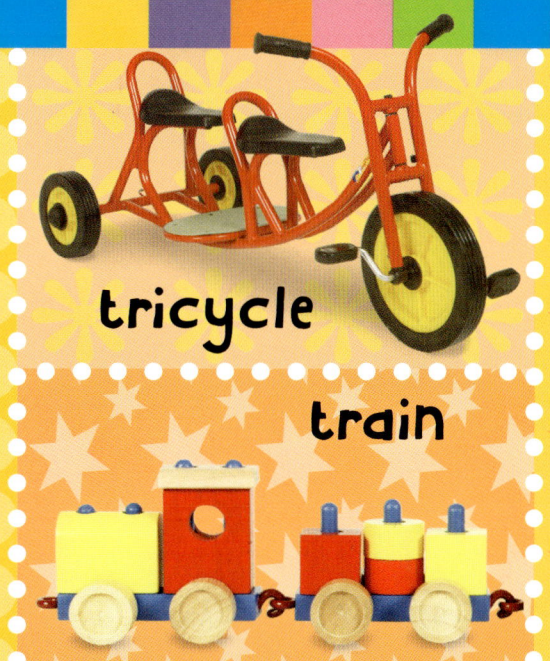

tricycle

doll

train

jigsaw

teddy bear

balloons

bat

ball

kite

dinosaur

blocks

Kitchen

A **kitchen** is the room where food is stored and prepared. Kitchens usually contain a refrigerator, cupboards, a sink and a stove.

biscuit cutters

apron

sieve

rolling pin

frying pan

saucepan

oven

fork

plate

spoon

knife

Home

Your **home** is the place where you live. Most homes have a kitchen, a living room, and one or more bedrooms and bathrooms.

chair

chest of drawers

bed

lamp

fireplace

table

bath

sofa

Garden

A **garden** is a place where people grow flowers and vegetables. A person's garden is usually next to their house.

seedling

watering can

ants

trowel

flower

boots

acorn

spider

snail

petal

stem

frog

Family

A **family** is a group of people who are related to each other. Most families have parents, children, and grandchildren.

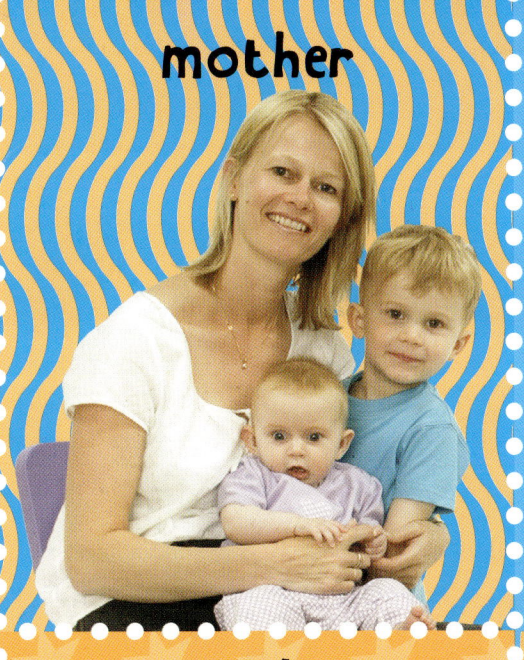

mother

sister

grandfather

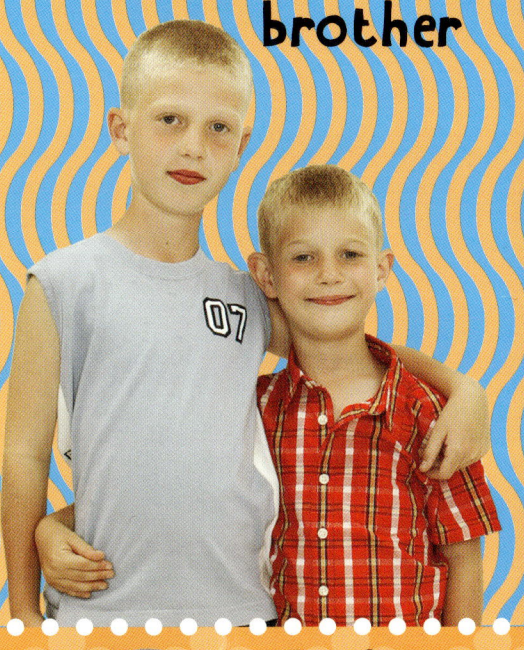

aunty

brother

grandmother

cousin

father

Clothes

Clothes are things that people wear.

scarf	hat	gloves
shorts	pants	shirt
	pyjamas	
dress	boots	shoes

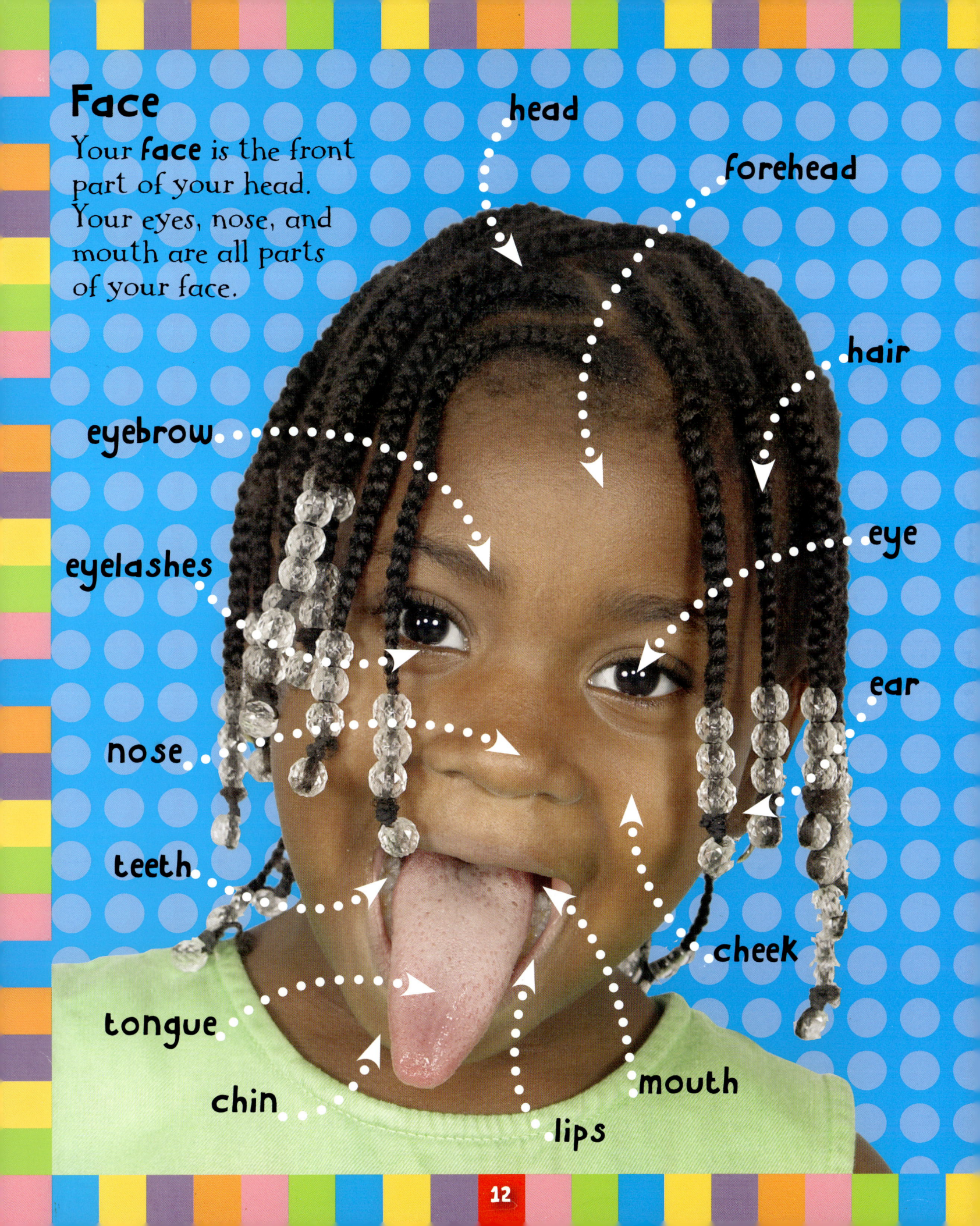

Face

Your **face** is the front part of your head. Your eyes, nose, and mouth are all parts of your face.

head

forehead

hair

eyebrow

eye

eyelashes

ear

nose

teeth

cheek

tongue

mouth

chin

lips

face
arm
hand
chest
stomach
hips
thigh
knee
leg
calf
shin
ankle
foot
heel

Body

Your **body** is every part of you, from your head to your toes. The different parts of your body work together to keep you alive and healthy.

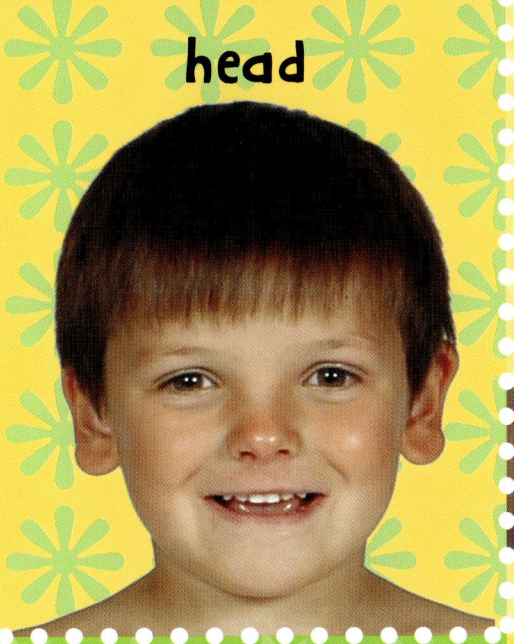

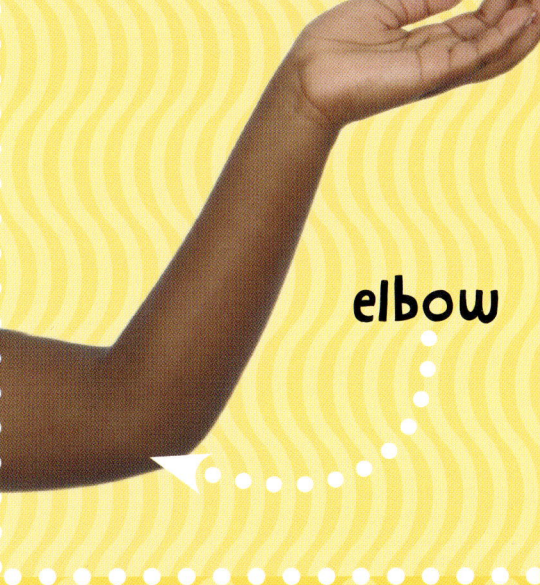

head

elbow

neck

finger

thumb

shoulder

toe

back

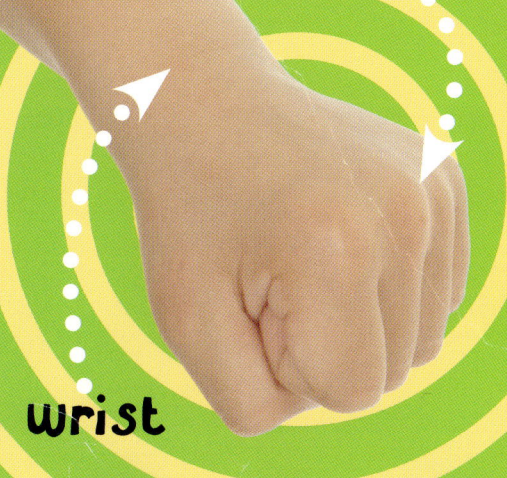

bottom

knuckles

wrist

Vegetables

A **vegetable** is part of a plant that is used for food. Peas, beans, cabbages, potatoes, cauliflowers, and onions are all vegetables.

carrot

potato

cabbage

pepper

onion

tomato

leek

broccoli

cauliflower

sweetcorn

cucumber

peas

Fruit

A **fruit** is the part of a plant that holds the seeds. Many fruits are juicy and delicious to eat.

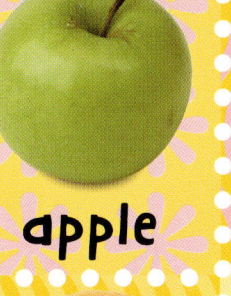

grapes

apple

lemon

orange

starfruit

pineapple

banana

melon

peach

pumpkin

strawberry

raspberry

Food

Food is anything that you eat to help you grow and keep you healthy. Fruit, vegetables, rice, and bread are all food.

sandwich

pasta

pie

ice cream

nuts

cake

sausages

bread

cheese

chocolate

Insects

An **insect** is a small animal with six legs. An insect's body is divided into three parts. Many insects have wings.

fly

butterfly

wasp

bee

dragonfly

beetle

ladybird

grasshopper

caterpillar

ant

Birds

A **bird** is an animal with wings, feathers, and a beak. Most birds are able to fly.

eagle

penguin

swan

owl

pigeon

duck

hornbill

wing

tail

beak

foot

feathers

Pets

A **pet** is a tame animal that you look after, often in your home or garden.

tortoise

guinea pig

cat

pony

hamster

goldfish

macaw

rabbit

mouse

dog

Farm animals

People keep **farm animals** for their meat, for the milk or eggs they produce, and for their skin or fur.

goat

piglet

dog

chick

cockerel

horse

foal

pig

sheep

cow

Wild animals

Animals are known as **wild animals** if they move around freely in the oceans, in the air, or in the mountains, forests and fields.

lizard

snake

tiger

chimpanzee

crocodile

shark

elephant

lion

My 2 in 1 Picture Dictionary

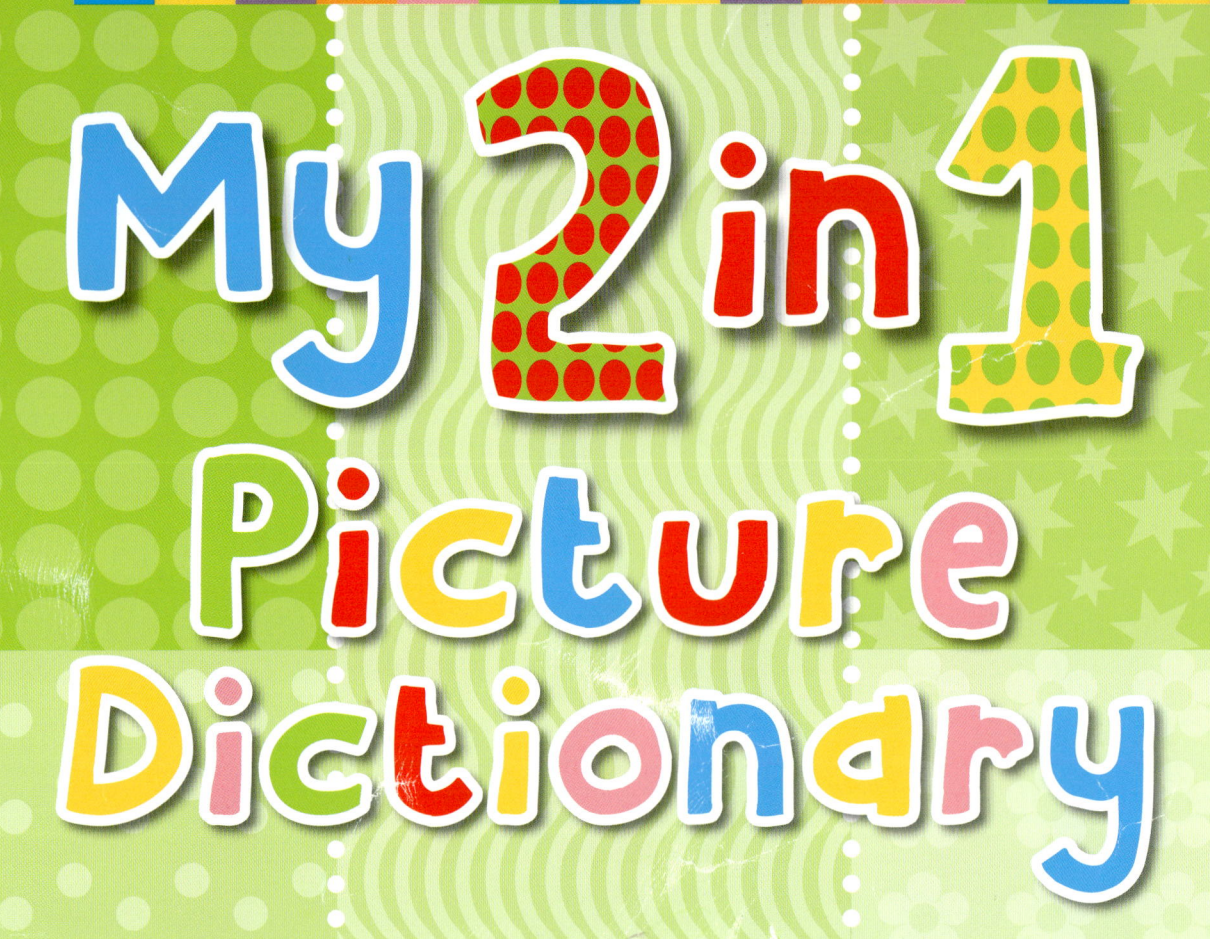

Thematic pages

With thanks to
Jane Horne and Helen Parker

Copyright © 2006
make believe ideas ltd
27 Castle Street, Berkhamsted,
Hertfordshire, HP4 2DW.

All rights reserved. No part of this publication may be reproduced, stored in a retrieval system, or transmitted in any form or by any means, electronic, mechanical, photocopying, recording, or otherwise, without the prior written permission of the copyright owner.
ISBN-10: 1-84610-131-x ISBN-13: 978 1 84610 131 1
Manufactured in Singapore.

make
believe
ideas